Drawing Cartoons from Numbers

Drawing Cartoons from Numbers

Create Fun Characters from 1 to 1001

 Get Creative 6

Christopher Hart Books for KIDS

An imprint of Get Creative 6
104 West 27th Street
New York, NY 10001

Editorial Director
JOAN KRELLENSTEIN

Managing Editor
LAURA COOKE

Senior Editor
MICHELLE BREDESON

Art Director
IRENE LEDWITH

Book Design
JULIE GRANT

Editorial Assistant
JACOB SEIFERT

Production
J. ARTHUR MEDIA

Vice President
TRISHA MALCOLM

Publisher
CAROLINE KILMER

Production Manager
DAVID JOINNIDES

Chairman
JAY STEIN

Library of Congress Cataloging-in-Publication Data
Hart, Christopher, 1957-
Drawing cartoons number by number : create fun characters from 1 to 1001 / Christopher Hart.
Description: First Edition. New York, NY : Drawing with Christopher Hart, 2017. Includes index.
Identifiers: LCCN 2017045278 | ISBN 9781640210127 (pbk.)
Subjects: LCSH: Numbers, Natural, in art--Juvenile literature. |Cartooning--Technique--Juvenile literature. | BISAC: JUVENILE NONFICTION / Art / Drawing.
Classification: LCC NC825.N86 H37 2018 | DDC 741.5/1--dc23
LC record available at https://lccn.loc.gov/2017045278
Printed in China.
3 5 7 9 10 8 6 4 2

• • •

christopherhartbooks.com

What's Inside

Drawing Is as Easy as 123!

Welcome, artists!

You can draw *zillions* of things by starting with a simple number. With some clear instruction and a little imagination, you can turn the number 3 into a bunny rabbit, make the number 4 into a fashion model, or even draw a dinosaur by starting with the number 5. I'll show you how! The steps are easy to follow—if you can draw a number, you can draw everything in this book. Use crayons or markers to add color to your

finished drawings to really make them stand out. With a little practice, you might even be inspired to transform a number into a cartoon of your own creation.

So grab a pencil and paper, pick out some lucky numbers, and get ready to have some drawing fun!

Happy Drawing!
Christopher Hart

NUMBERS 1-9

If you can write the numbers 1 through 9, you can draw

anything! Get started by saying hello to a friendly  or by

saying goodbye to a cheery . You can even take a winter

walk with a or have a chat with a  along the way. It's

the magic of cartooning. All it takes is a pencil and your imagination.

Let the magic begin!

Mr. Big Mouth

Friendly bear

Fashion sense

Absurd bird

My, what big teeth you have!

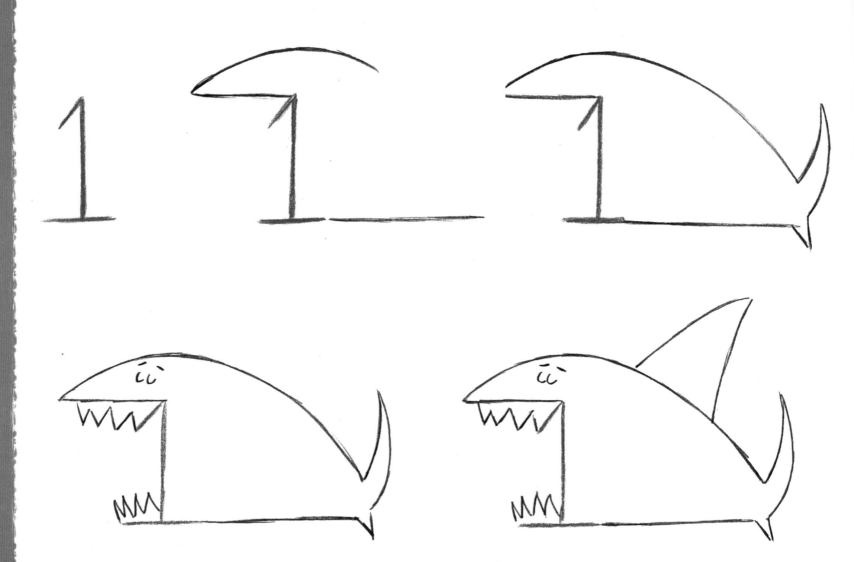

clueless dad

Fuzzy hedgehog

Squeezable penguin

1

All aboard

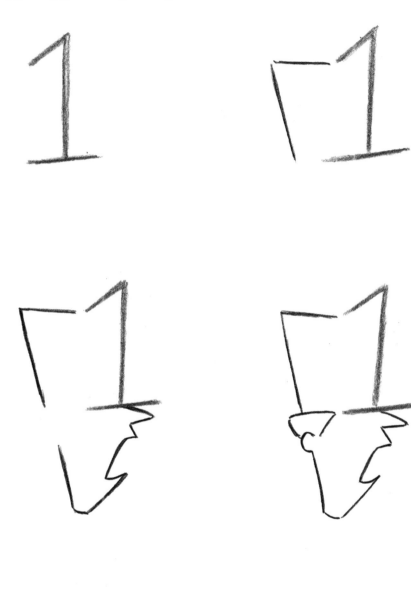

Koala confusion

23

Friendly frog

Duckling out for a swim

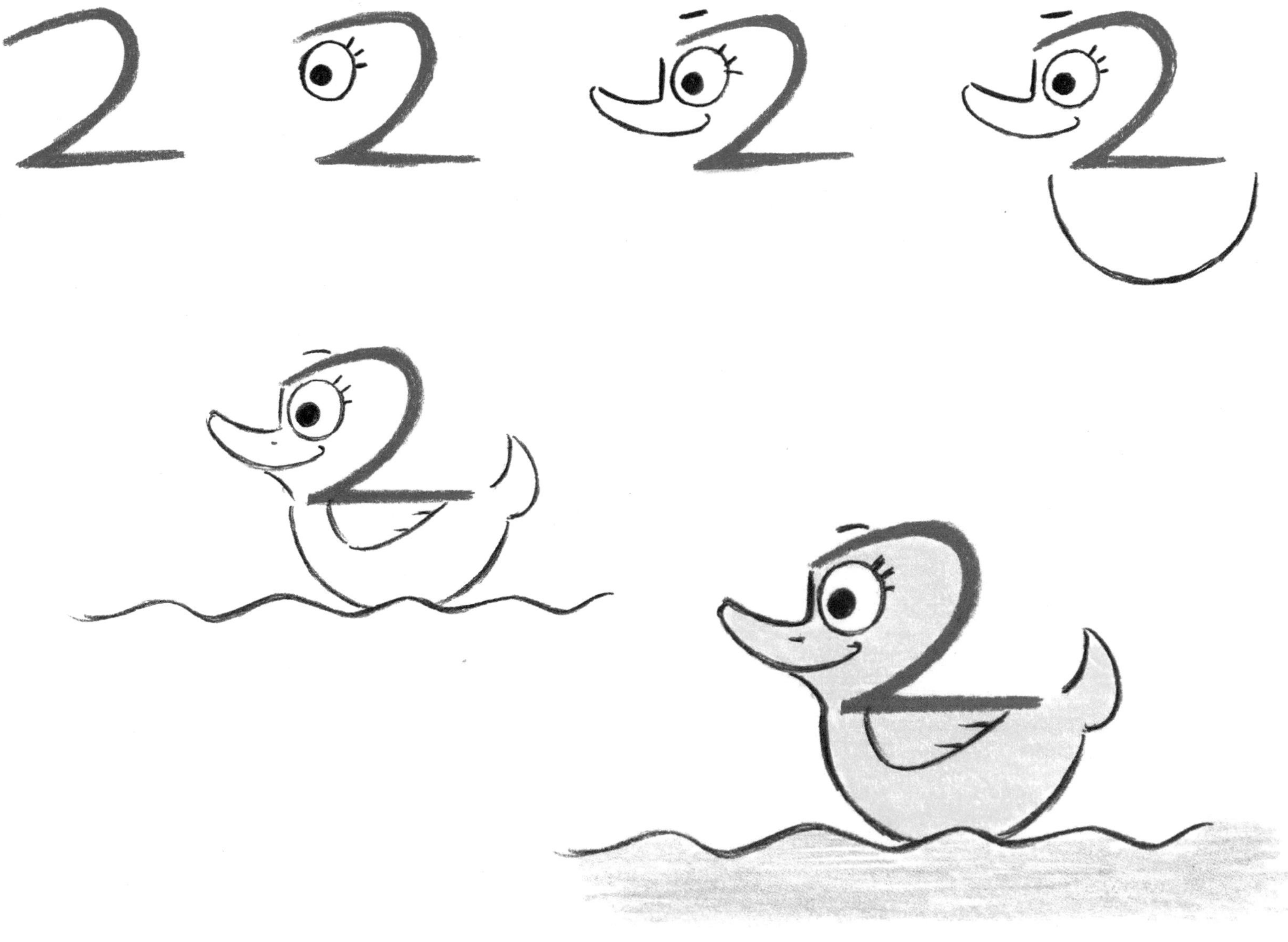

Hot sauce

Feeling good

2

Grrrrr-izzly bear

BOO!

Hound with a hunch

33

Beyond fluffy

Sparkling smile

Bear buddy

Cranky octopus

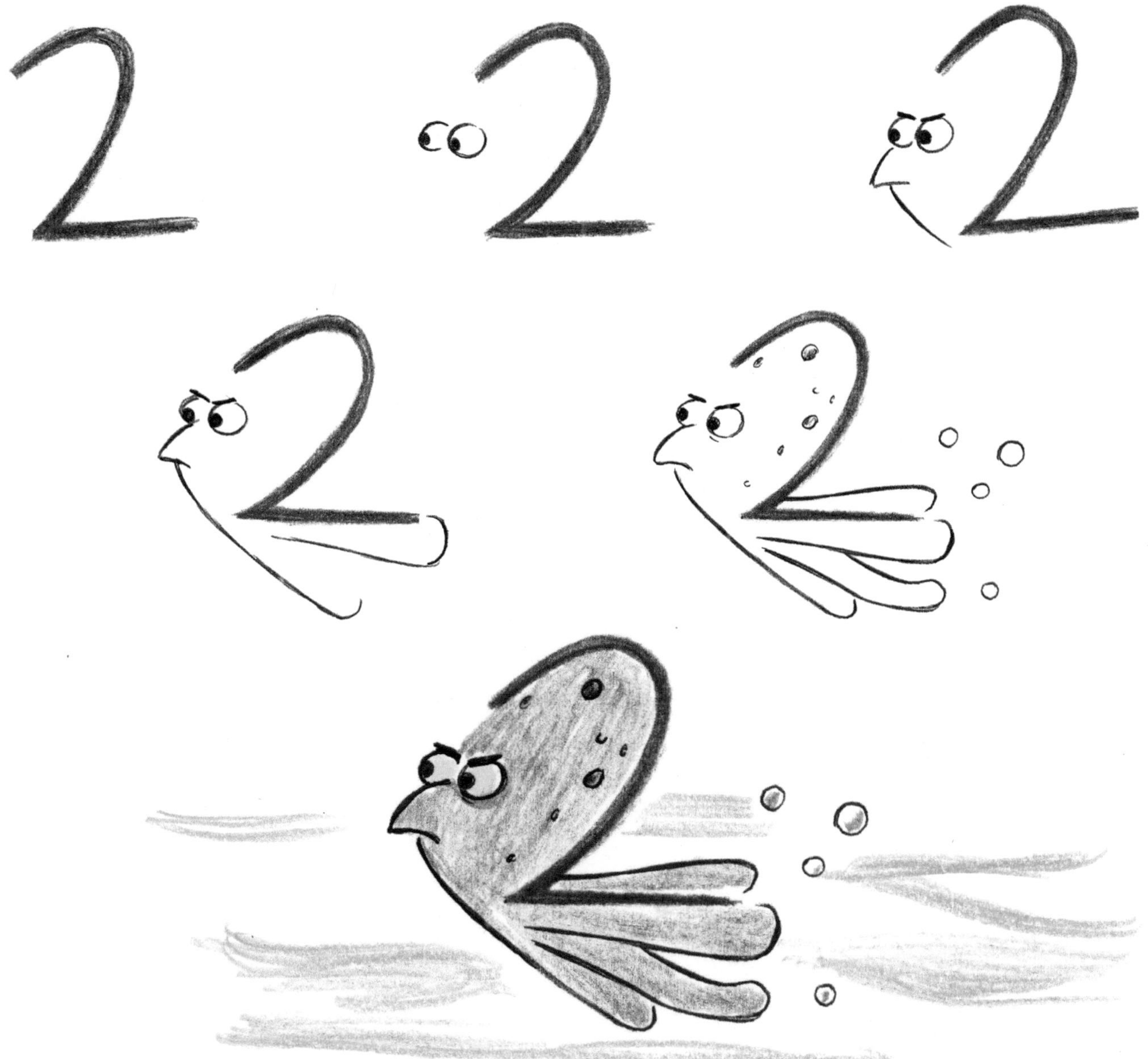

Batter up!

Perplexed armadillo

Friendly teen

Sunny bunny

Puppy

Dad with glasses

Hippo

Gushing girl

Witty kitty

Stylish drawing

Cowabunga

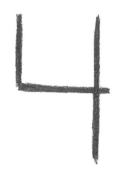

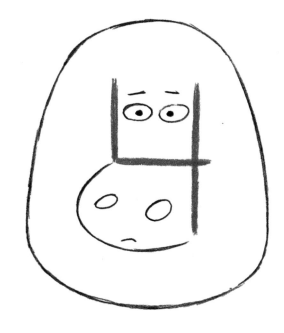

Wet weather forecast

Giraffe

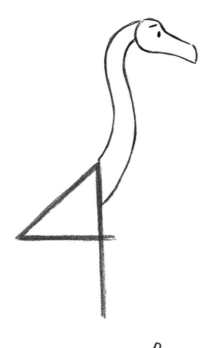

Well-mannered wolf

Magical guardian

Happy guy

Big smile

Stay!

Kid in a panic

Kooky bird

Chipmunk to the rescue!

Surprised bear

Sitting kitty

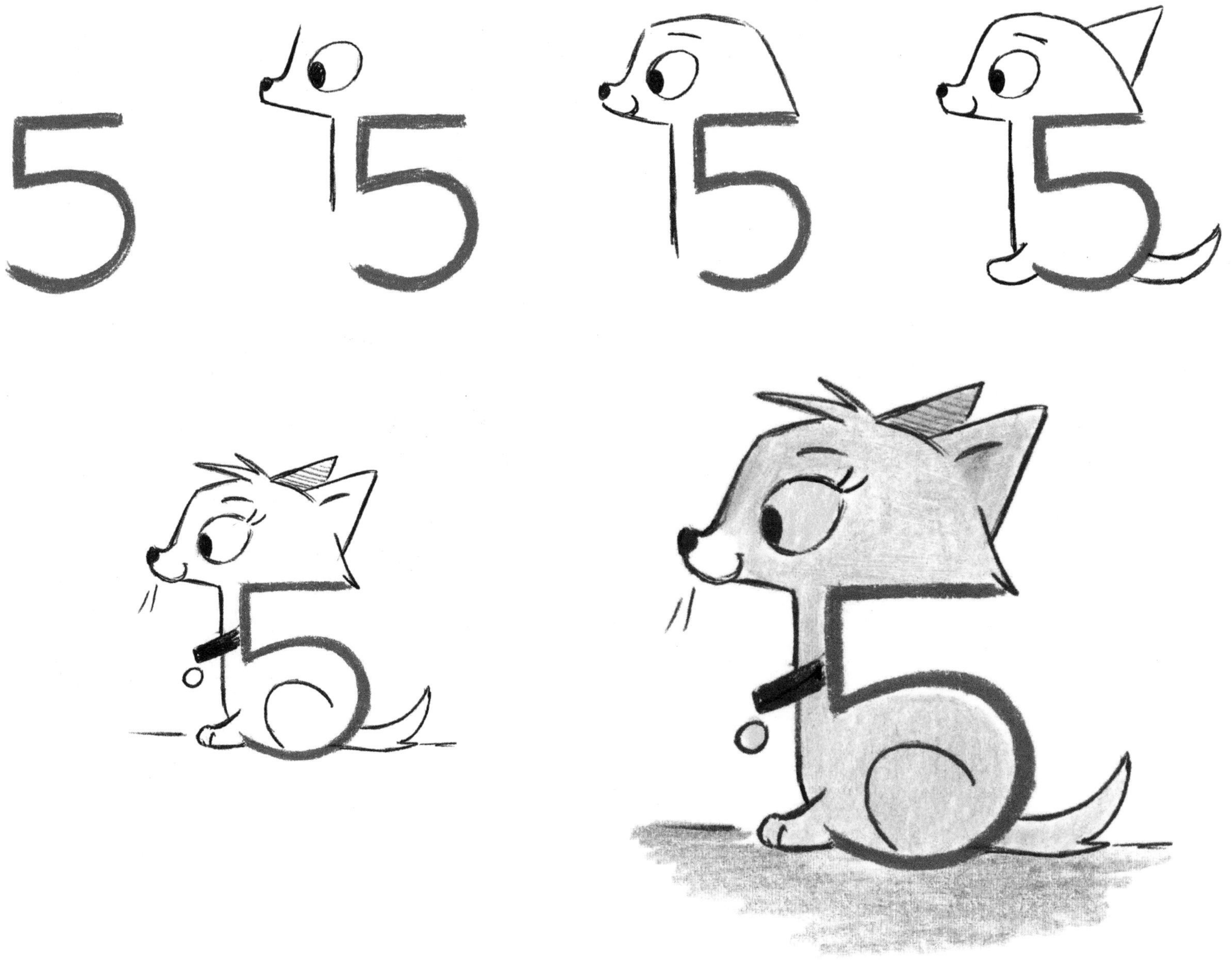

Tough to tackle

5 5 5 5

A friend with feathers

Lion with a big mane

5 5 5 5

Winter walk

Pterodactyl

Your order is ready!

Fun in the sun

The art of begging

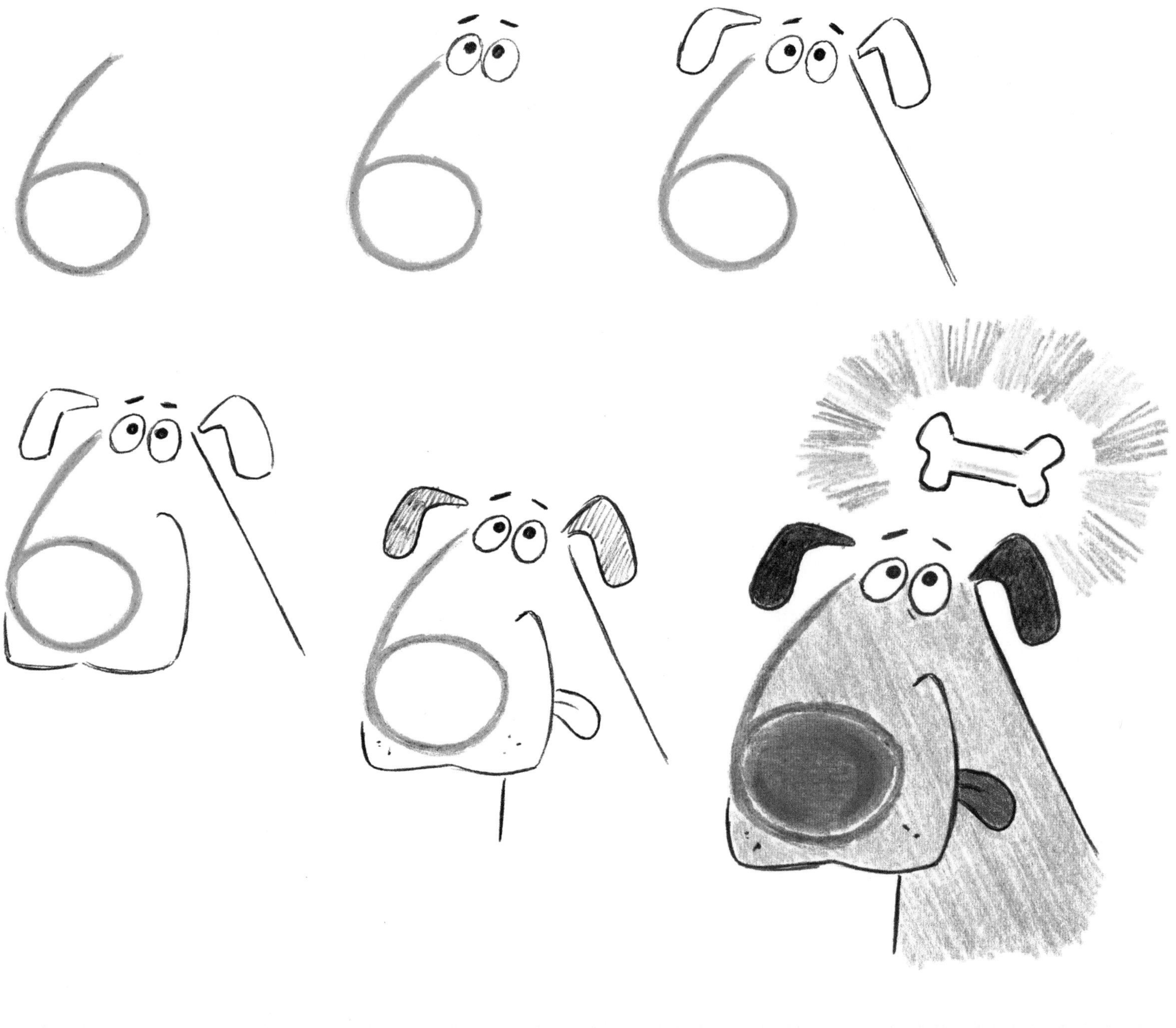

"Listen to this!"

Woodland fox

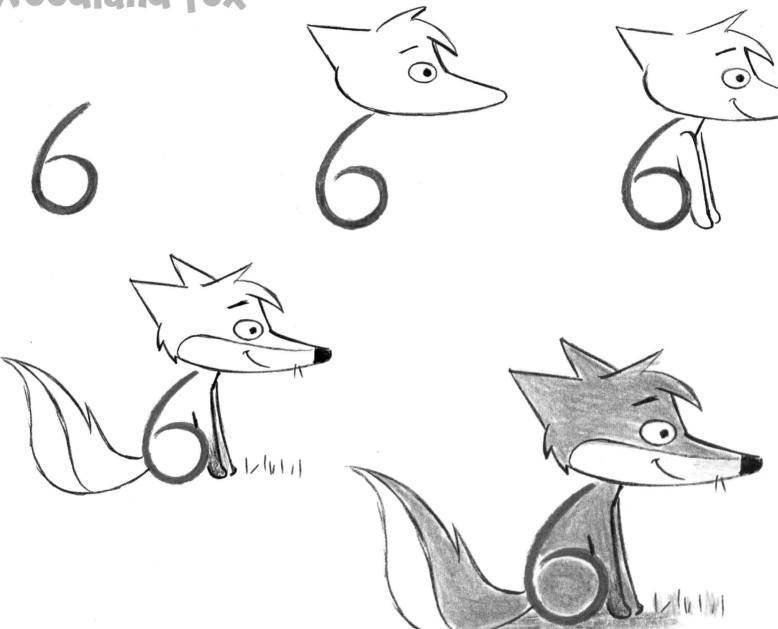

Snail

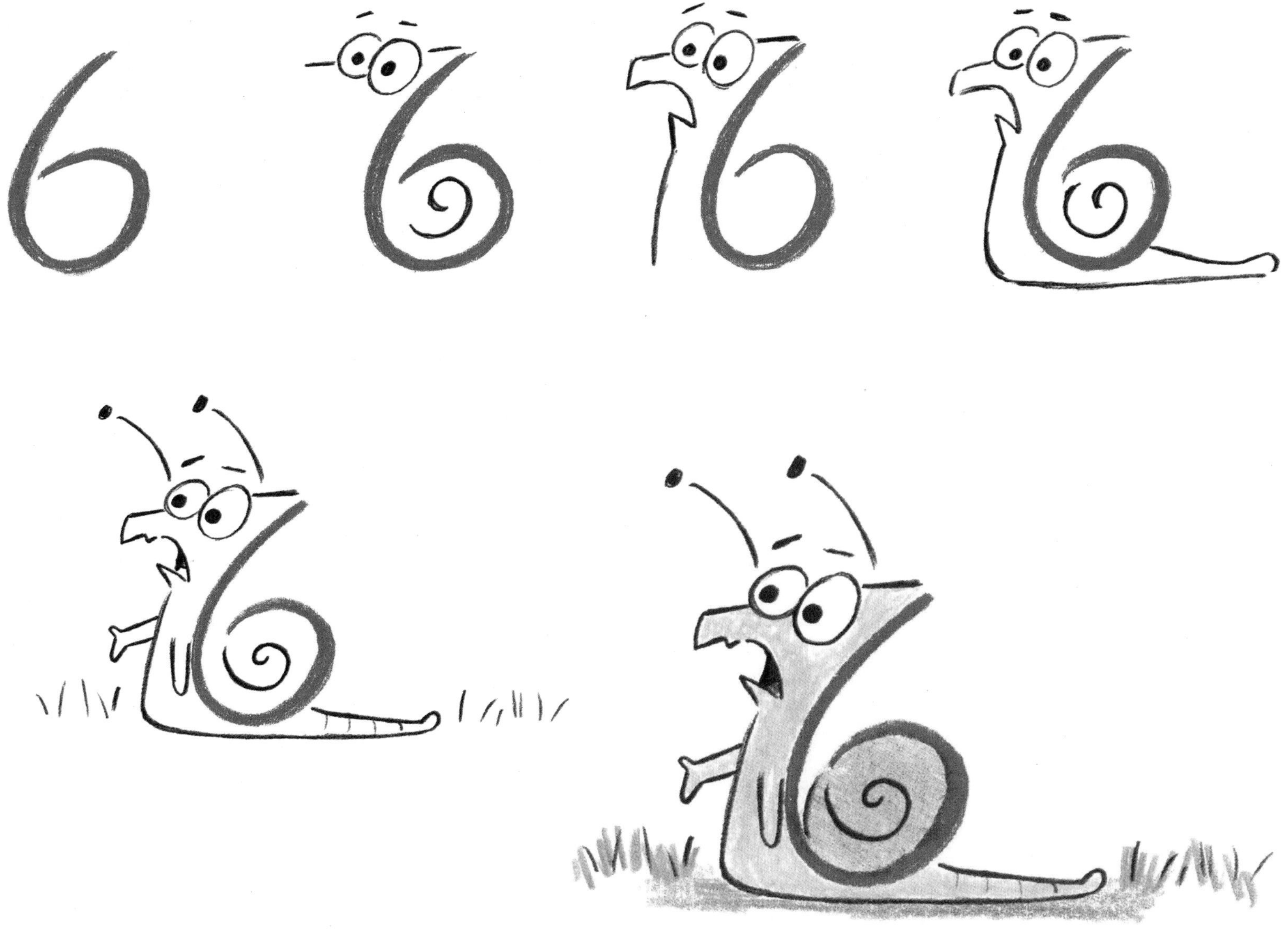

Worried warthog

A sense of humor

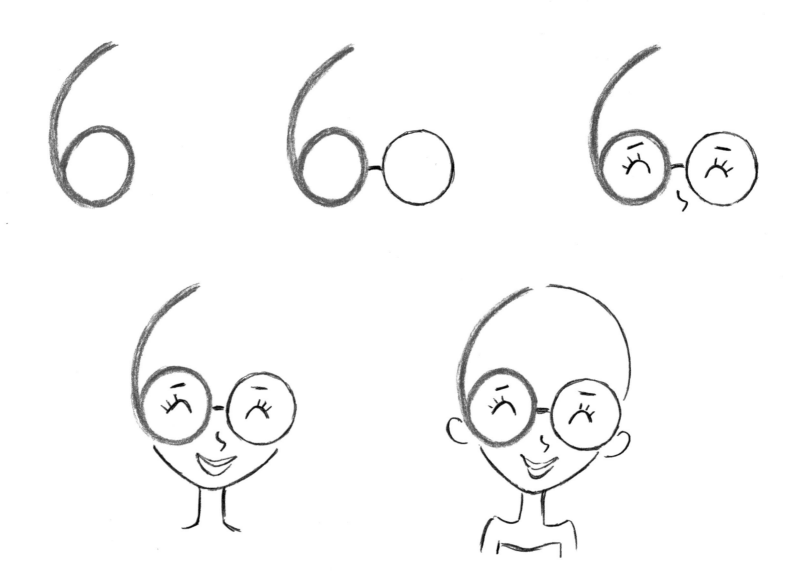

Just remembered something!

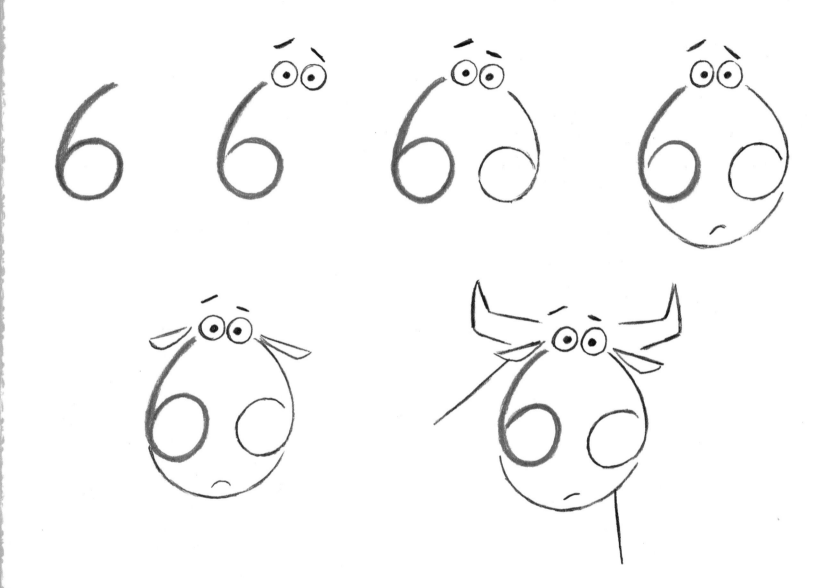

Curious bunny

Cheerful expression

Wolf

101

Chuckling bear

"No, and you can't make me!"

Is that cheese I see?

Pretty in pink

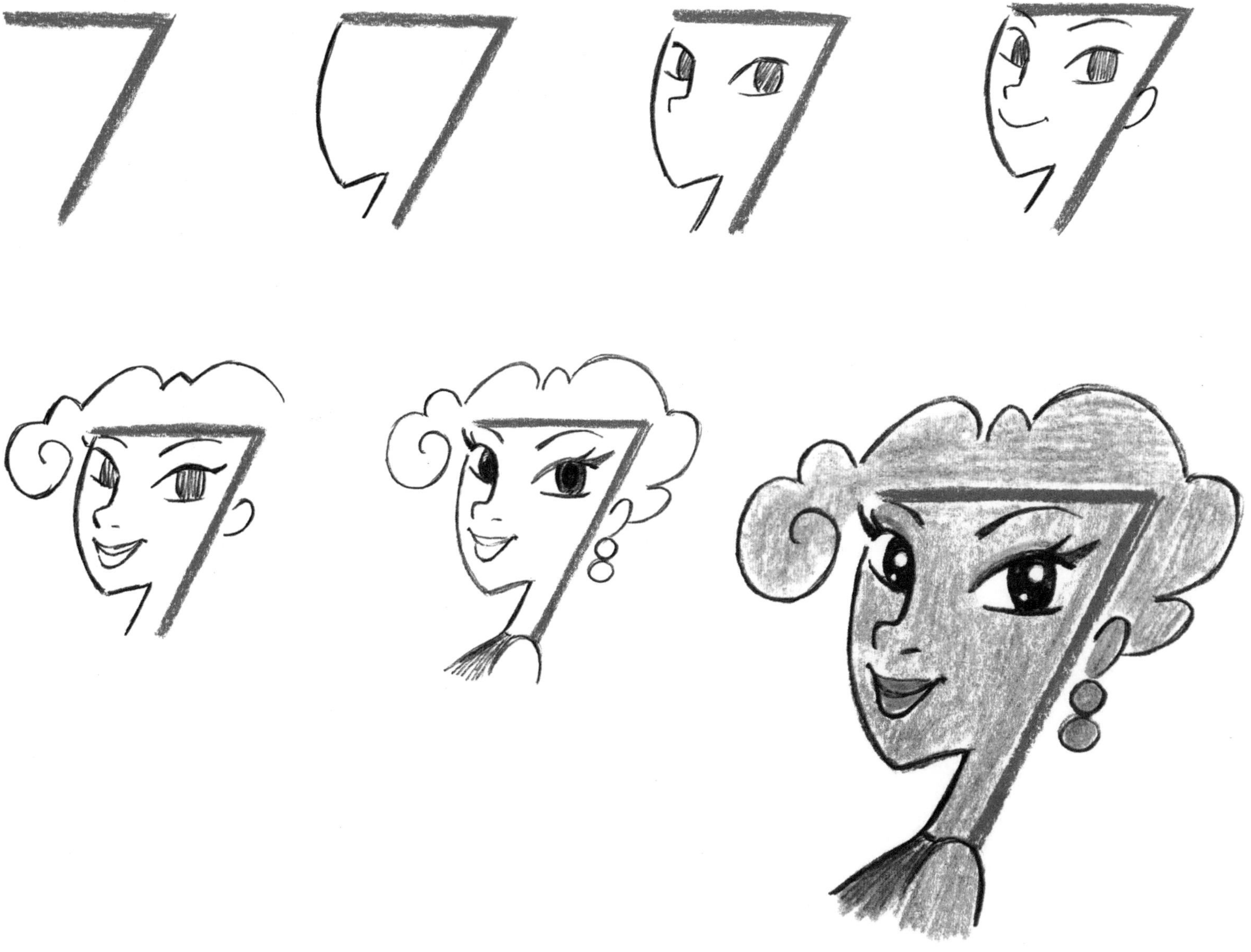

upbeat dad

Supercool

Fun haircut

Queen

Guilty puppy

Bug buddy

113

Cool penguin

Plump bear

Regal ruler

"Hi, got any extra brine shrimp?"

Bunny and egg

YUM!

YUM!

121

Crazy toon

"You can never get a human on these things!"

Got cow?

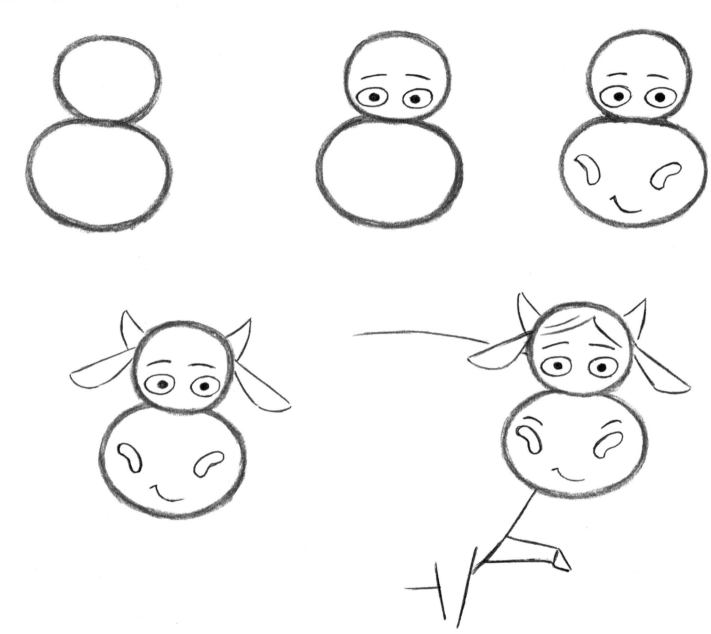

Big nose bear

Sharp profile

Smiling elephant

Basset hound

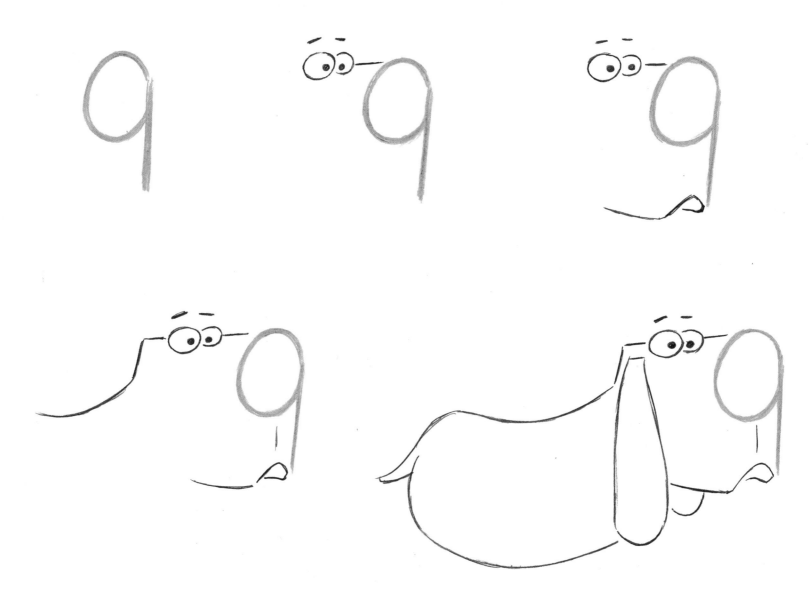

Big mouth

Happy doggy

Numbers 10-1001

Now let's make things a little more interesting by drawing characters

starting with two numbers. First, we'll count off by tens—you'll learn how to

turn the number 10 into a simple , transform the number

20 into a little , or make an imposing from

the number 30, etc. Then we'll begin to explore random double-digits as

examples of the funny characters you can draw starting with just about any

number combination. There are no limits to what you can create!

Bird

Little fish

Mean guy

Chicken

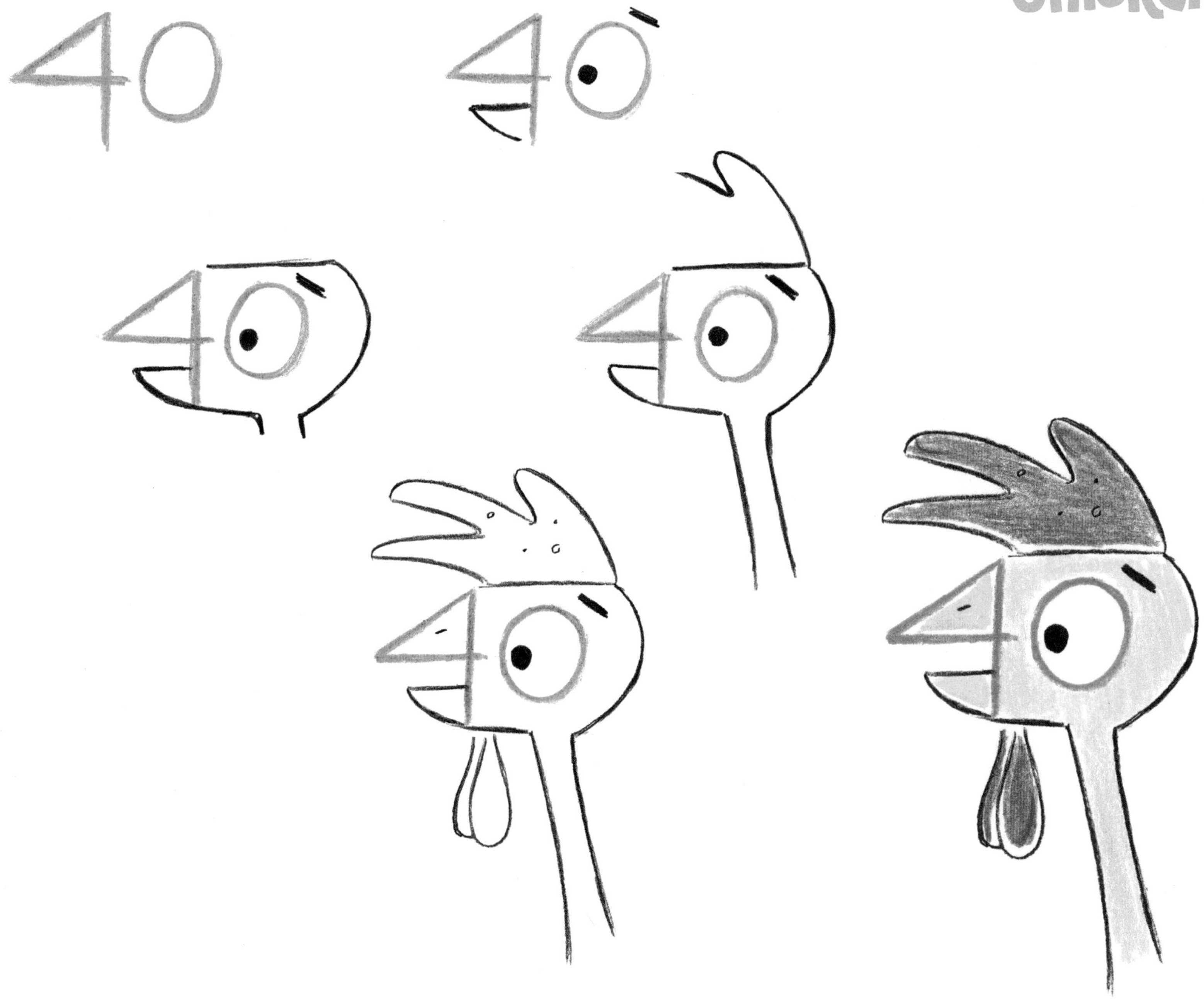

Bull

5o

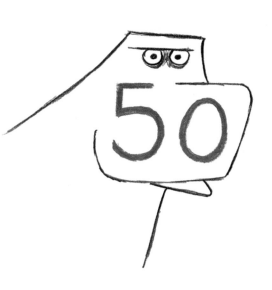

Oh no!

Hero

Good-mood monkey

Funny guy

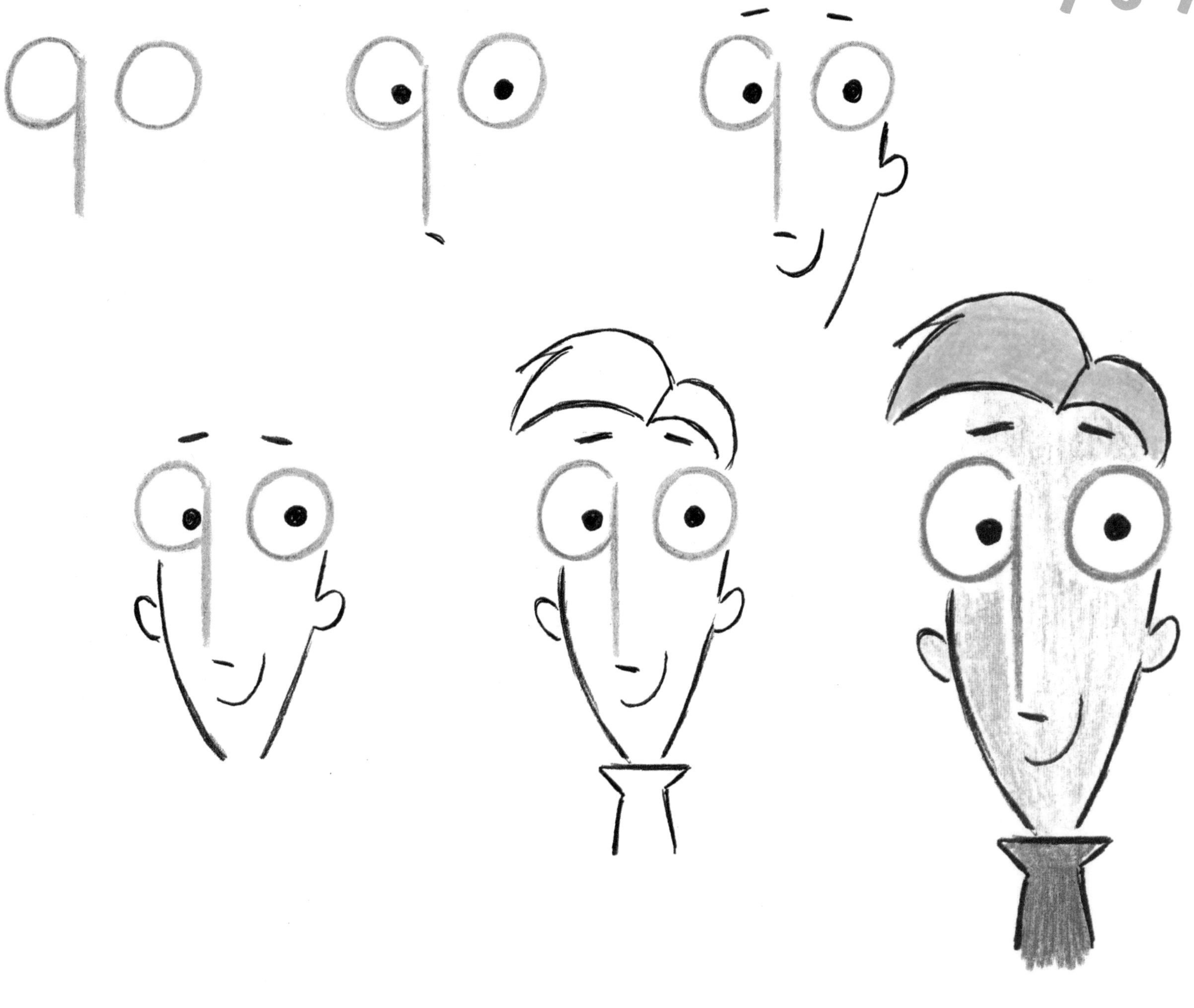

Crocodile

100   100

Crabby

Oops!

Mom and daughter kangaroo

Bear getting somewhere

Puppy in trouble!

25   25   25

25   25

Conquistador

Bunny with a snack

Glad dad

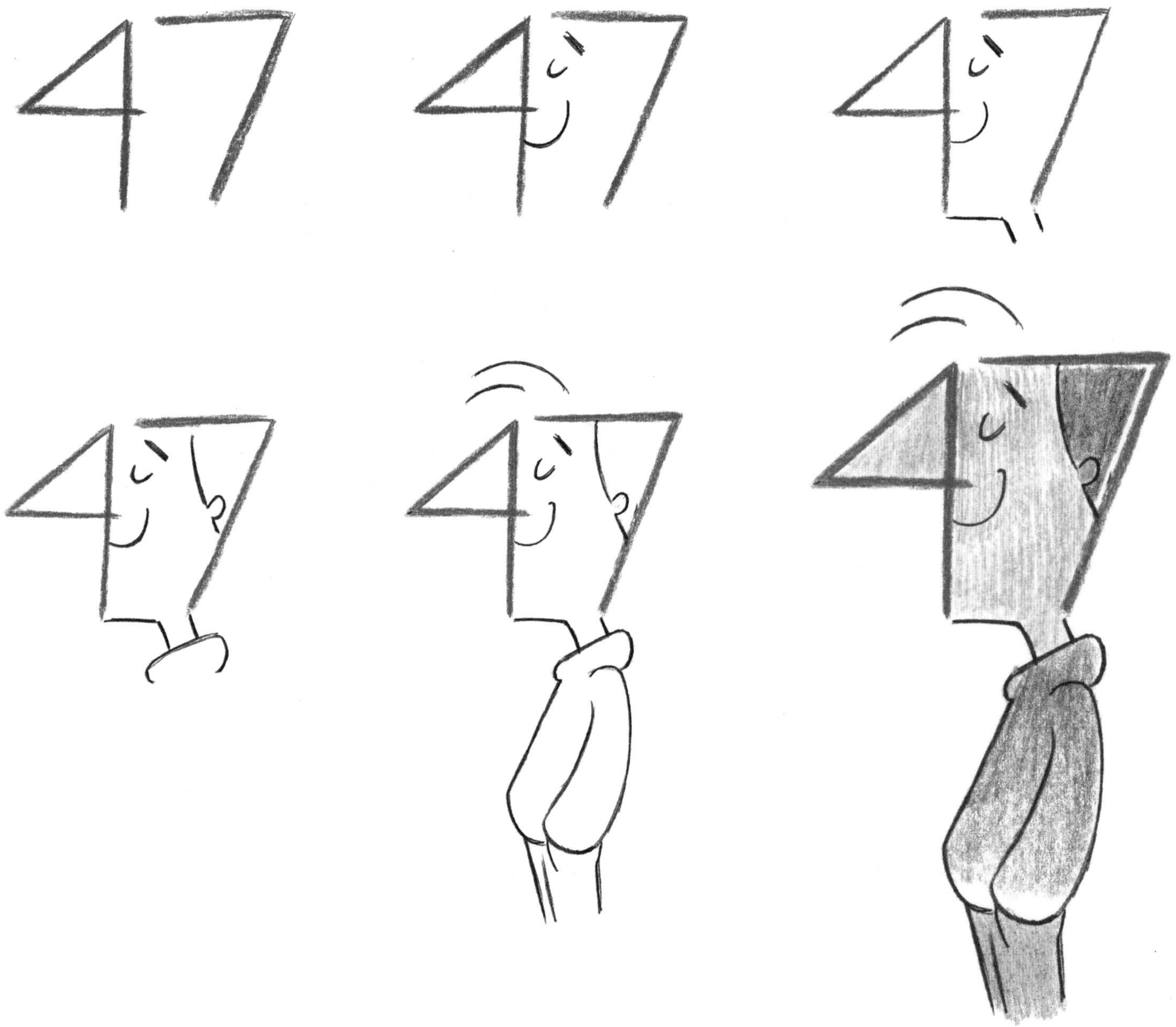

"What do you mean we're going extinct?"

Porcupine

Quirky glasses

Panting pooch

WOOF!

Squeezable chipmunk

607

Raccoon

Looking for your favorite character?
Check the alphabetical list to see which page it's on.

Love DRAWING with NUMBERS?
TRY DRAWING with SIMPLE SHAPES anD LeTTeRS!

Connect with Chris on YouTube at www.youtube.com/chrishartbooks.
Available wherever books are sold.